D0842482

Pebble™

Weather

Snow

by Helen Frost

Consulting Editor: Gail Saunders-Smith, Ph.D.
Consultant: Joseph M. Moran, Ph.D., Meteorologist
Associate Director, Education Program
American Meteorological Society
Washington, D.C.

Capstone
Mankato, Minnesota

Pebble Books are published by Capstone Press
151 Good Counsel Drive, P.O. Box 669, Mankato, Minnesota 56002
www.capstonepress.com

1 2 3 4 5 6 09 08 07 06 05 04

Library of Congress Cataloging-in-Publication Data
Frost, Helen, 1949–
  Snow / by Helen Frost.
  p. cm.—(Weather)
  Summary: Simple text and photographs present snow, how it is formed,
and how it affects the Earth and people.
  Includes bibliographical references and index.
  ISBN 0-7368-2095-7 (hardcover) 3021-9389 -304
  1. Snow—Juvenile literature. [1. Snow.] I. Title. II. Series: Weather
(Mankato, Minn.)
QC926.37.F75 2004
551.57′84—dc22
                                                             2003013406

Note to Parents and Teachers

The Weather series supports national science standards related
to earth science. This book describes and illustrates snow. The
photographs support early readers in understanding the text.
The repetition of words and phrases helps early readers learn new
words. This book also introduces early readers to subject-specific
vocabulary words, which are defined in the Glossary. Early readers
may need assistance to read some words and to use the Table of
Contents, Glossary, Read More, Internet Sites, and Index/Word List
sections of the book.

Table of Contents

What Is Snow?

Snow is cold and soft. Snow sometimes piles up on the ground. Snow sometimes melts on the ground.

6

Ice crystals form out
of water vapor when the
air is cold. Water vapor
is an invisible gas.
Ice crystals gather together
to form snowflakes.

8

Snowflakes fall from clouds.
Each snowflake is different.
Snowflakes have many
shapes. Most snowflakes
have six sides.

Types of Snow

Some snow is soft and dry. It feels like powder. People ski or sled on it.

Some snow is wet.

Wet snow sticks together.

People make snowmen and snowballs out of it.

Blizzards are windy snowstorms. People cannot see through blizzards. Cars can become stuck in deep snow.

What Snow Does

Snow covers the ground like a blanket. Even though snow is cold, it keeps the ground warm.

People and animals leave
tracks when they walk
in snow. Each person
and each animal leaves
a different track.

20

Melting

Snow melts when the weather is warm. Melted snow becomes water. The water soaks into the ground or runs off into streams. The snow disappears.

Glossary

blizzard—a heavy snowstorm with strong wind; a blizzard can last several days.

crystal—a solid substance having a regular pattern of many flat surfaces; snowflakes are made of ice crystals.

freeze—to change from a liquid to a solid; water freezes at 32 degrees Fahrenheit (0 degrees Celsius).

melt—to change from a solid to a liquid; snow melts above 32 degrees Fahrenheit (0 degrees Celsius).

snowflake—many ice crystals that are clumped together

vapor—a gas; water can be a gas, a liquid, or a solid.

Read More

Frost, Helen. *Water as a Solid*. Water. Mankato, Minn.: Pebble Books, 2000.

Schaefer, Lola M. *A Snowy Day*. What Kind of Day Is It? Mankato, Minn.: Pebble Books, 2000.

Sherman, Josepha. *Flakes and Flurries: A Book about Snow*. Amazing Science. Minneapolis: Picture Window Books, 2003.

Internet Sites

FactHound offers a safe, fun way to find Internet sites related to this book. All of the sites on FactHound have been researched by our staff.

Here's how:

1. Visit *www.facthound.com*

2. Type in this special code **0736820957** for age-appropriate sites. Or enter a search word related to this book for a more general search.

3. Click on the **Fetch It** button.

FactHound will fetch the best sites for you!

Index/Word List

animals, 19
blizzards, 15
cars, 15
clouds, 9
cold, 5, 7, 17
disappears, 21
dry, 11
ice crystals, 7
invisible, 7

melts, 5, 21
people, 11,
  13, 15, 19
piles, 5
powder, 11
ski, 11
sled, 11
snowflake,
  7, 9

snowstorms,
  15
soft, 5, 11
track, 19
warm, 17, 21
water, 21
water vapor, 7
weather, 21
wet, 13

Word Count: 169
Early-Intervention Level: 18

Editorial Credits
Martha E. H. Rustad, editor; Timothy Halldin, series designer; Molly Nei, book
   designer; Deirdre Barton, photo researcher; Karen Risch, product planning editor

Photo Credits
Bruce Coleman Inc./Gary Withey, 20
Corbis, 8, 16; Chuck Savage, 12; Marc Muench, cover
Index Stock Imagery/Vloo Phototheque, 10
Steve Mulligan, 1
Unicorn Stock Photos/B. W. Hoffman, 4; Charlie Schmidt, 6; David P. Dill, 18;
   Mark E. Gibson, 14

The author thanks the children's library staff at the Allen County Public Library in
Fort Wayne, Indiana, for research assistance.